Poetr

A fundraising poetry collection,
life's rich offerings.
Created with love by Anita Williams

Happy reading!
Love & best wishes
from
Anita x

Dedications:-

Cover design by Emma Wellings

Thank you Emma, for producing a wonderful cover for this very special book xx

Thank you to Simon, Amy and Dan for supporting me throughout this writing journey x

A Fundraising Book

This is a fundraising poetry collection for the Midlands Air Ambulance Charity, which is the only charity responsible for funding and operating three air ambulances across six Midland counties in England.

The vital service is 100 per cent funded by the generosity of the general public and local businesses across the communities it serves, and since 1991 the charity has undertaken over 40,000 air ambulance missions.

Author's note

Hello there. If you are reading this note, then you've probably already got an inkling that you have made a difference by purchasing something very special! You have assisted in raising funds for a very worthy cause indeed, so let me start by saying a heartfelt thank you!

Once I had decided to write a poetry book to boost funds for the Midlands Air Ambulance Charity, I thought about the content carefully. It didn't take me long to determine that I needed to know more about them, what they do, and how they go about their missions. So, when these wonderful people invited me to their base at RAF Cosford, I jumped at the chance!

I was greeted with the friendliest of welcomes and talked first with Richard, a doctor who flies on the missions. He talked passionately to me about the complexities of dealing with patients in difficult surroundings, and how rewarding it is to get to the scene fast, so that lives are actually saved. Along with a team of superb paramedics, these guys go out in tricky weather conditions to tend to the wounded and the sick, working in remote and dangerous areas in an effort to get the job done.

Moving on to a chat with Tim, a Pilot, who flies in extreme conditions at times. I was enthralled to learn of how intricate the helicopter landings are... from valleys with overhead power cables, to motorways with intrusive overhead lights, to city situations where the recirculating air above tall buildings can play havoc with the rota blades. Maps are seriously important, and as I glanced next to the passenger front seat, I could see a carefully organised box of maps. Tim explained that once they have determined the 'A' to 'B,' a line is ruled across the map. he called it his "Roman road in the sky." Getting as close to the patient as possible is their number one goal, as valuable seconds really do help.

I told them they were heroes, and I was really taken aback by their response. They told me that I was a hero too! They wouldn't be able to run their missions without fundraising, indeed they are 100% funded by the generosity of fundraisers who understand what needs to be done to get them in the air.

Well… with a reaction like that, you can imagine how motivated I have now become to get this book right, and Richard and Tim inspired me to write a poem about the charity itself which is included in this book, entitled "Heroes of the Golden Hour."

The mixture of poems in this book have been lovingly created over many years and I have selected a variety of topics in an effort to include something for everyone, plus the inclusion of many fresh new poems exclusively for this publication.

I hope, upon reading, that you will soon feel at home amongst the pages of rhymes and poems which have been written to give you a lift and make you smile as most poems are heart warming and carry a positive message.

Writing this book has been a rewarding experience and I am delighted to donate a percentage of the revenue from the sale of every 'Poetry Giving' book to this extraordinary charity.

Anita Williams

Heroes of the golden hour

You can ponder as a poet, as you try to find the words…
Just how can you describe this team who fly up with the birds?
Tireless commitment as the blades take to the sky
Preparing for each moment takes precision; honed to try.
Up against all weathers, as they search for cleaner air
Every mission helps a life, epitomising care.
On the scene this golden hour, the maps laid out to guide
Pilots, paramedics and the doc's prepared inside.
Identify location, they've got the 'long and lat'
Draw a line across the map to where the patient's sat.
Straight line's drawn, they're on their way, to deal with who knows what
The Roman road across the sky; Search hard for landing spot.
Saving lives, this awesome team, deserving of all praise
One hundred per cent funded by good folk in many ways.
Those who give up time to care are heroes alongside
The crew and Maac the mascot; all committed and with pride.
All living with a purpose, don't leave anything to chance
Let's get behind and rally for this flying Ambulance.
And as the blades get closer to each place they need to stop
Emotions ease and trust we will, those heroes as they drop.
Professionals with hearts perform their duty; time to spare,
And if you ever need them, they will all take to the air.

Contents

Sunflower

Breezes capture dancing heads
Compacted seeds all singing
Sun kissing golden petals edge
Florist trug we're bringing.
We make selection, just a few
We don't disturb them all
Shop window now, display anew
Head and shoulders stand so tall.
But it's in the fields their glory shows
Their freedom better suited
Appreciate this feast for eyes
Majestic, convoluted.'
Tangled stems in tune so well,
Faces turn to sun
Unique and quirky circles swell
At sunshine beam's warm run.
Ablaze these fields of nature's jewels
Capture hearts this finest hour
Applaud our senses for this sight
Magnificent sunflower.

Kingfisher

Feathers resplendent in aquamarine
Proud and important, the Kingfisher's preen.
He waits with a razor sharp eye for his prey
And dives through the fortress of rapids and spray.
His catch is abundant; not one fish, but two
On his perch his magnificence radiates blue.
Nature's finest precision at work as he fishes
A lightening bolt of turquoise, then wriggles and squishes.
Out of the water as fast as he came
Safe harvest on riverbank, then off for the same.
Once fatted this gluttonous plumage flies on
A dart of emotional splendour.....then gone.

The Dancer

Rhythm always evident
No matter where he goes
Even sitting silently
You'll notice tapping toes
The music is his lifeblood
And every waking tick
His mind is on the dance floor
Where his moves are fluid; slick.
Gliding over pavements
To sounds that beckon him
The click of nifty fingers
Gets him moving every limb.
The dancer is exquisite
And exacting of his art
The precision of his motion
Leaves us breathless from the start.

For the breath of a dragon

This mystical beast Provides aura and charm
No boundaries for the legend of fable,
I'll quantify all that I have in a heartbeat
And summon the strength, if I am able,
To see through the eyes of one so sure
A confidence rush till his prey leaves his door.
His territory marked, his presence sublime
Speckled flesh full of scales; moves like poetry, rhyme.
Muscles unrivalled, talons from the mind
Of his imaginative creators, beloved mankind.
We talk of his victories, and those who'd been slain
We tell tales of brave warriors who fight through the pain.
This magical creature who lives in us all
Can be called upon anytime we conjure the call.
Beckon the moment: arched back full of spikes
His wingspan magnificent, surveys o'er our hikes.
His mouth full of razor sharp teeth, glistened hue
Look out for this monster of myth, and be true.
Through nostrils he snorts, billows pre cursor smoke,
And the fire that follows from hot breath is no joke.
With passion and fury, this imprint that smarts,
Behold ye, the Dragon, he's captured our hearts.

Ripples

Raindrops plop quietly, a few, and then more,
As the lake laps so gracefully close to the shore.
Ripples cause candy stripes all in a row,
And skies create atmosphere, sun giving glow.
As rain travels over, away from the scene,
Waters are still again, calm and serene.
Soon there is laughter and voices are heard,
The crisp air so peaceful, detects every word:-
'Let's send us some spinners out over the top."
Pebbles fly 'cross the water, relentless, then stop!
Culprits move on, and blurring their wake,
Kaleidoscope ripples glisten and shake.
Circles decreasing like diamonds in sun,
Captivate moments for thinkers who come.
To contemplate issues or troubles or love,
And everyday thoughts as they draw from above.
All of the feelings they hold best and dear,
The water's their sanctuary, rested and clear.
Ducks bob and the boatmen, they ripple some more,
Each giving us something that's worth waiting for
A pattern, a picture, like poetry, right there,
No wonder we love by the lakeside to stare.

Cloud pictures

From flows of cotton trailing high
My mind makes pictures in the sky
Empty other cluttered thought
And concentrate, sanctuary sought.
A crocodile! And a cove I see
These wonders staring down at me.
Blades of grass cradle my face
As herds of Lipizzaners race
And heart shapes fade revealing sun
With shadows cast, there's more to come.
A unicorn, a curly snake
My senses now all wide awake
Imagination stirs the soul
I'm loving this overloading bowl
Of consciousness with love at fore
Look hard again, and then there's more.
A tortoise? What's that telling me?
Slow down and ponder: all to see
Complexity a distant blur
This peaceful moment's tonic spur.
A cloak with tassels floats around
Then gently settles on the ground
Horizon giving helping hand
To fantasy, till I finally stand.
Fulfilled with thanks, this fleeting charm
Brightened my day, and gave me calm.

Key's tapestry

I'm staring so hard, at this polished old key.
Well used and with history, but why come to me?
Intriguing and battered, so where does it live?
A lock's to be opened, so come on key, give!
Spill beans, your existence, from where does it stem?
I've bunches of other keys but you're not one of them
What tapestry has been woven, what's your family tree?
Could it be that for ever you're a mystery?
Do I leave you for now, in a drawer there to sit
Or do I take action and get on with it?
I'm brimming to bursting point now; who are you?
There are so many answers for me to chew through.
So many options: a bank vault, a door?
Oh all this excitement just makes me want more,
Imagination is dangerous at times such as this,
Think long and hard I say, try not to miss.
Scrape the barrel of history, scour the past.
This key belongs somewhere, list of options now vast,
Or should I give up now and just leave it be?
Is it right that I to question it's journey to me?
I'll bask in this mystery, riotous imagining my spur,
If there's a lock out there somewhere, let's have fate right the blur.

Lantern's Glow

Dusk invites an ambience
A mood for us to make
Casting shadows over living space
Romantic allure at stake.
Candles shimmer gently
Casting wafts as people pass
The lantern's glow shines warmly
Dancing embers through the glass
Reflecting happy faces
Contented looks abound this eve
Maximising what we have
A calming sheen the flickers weave.

Fisherman

With water thigh deep, sure footed he stands,
All around him is quiet, save birdsong and the slow current ripple.
The fisherman has no plans today,
His place is here, at peace with the morning.
With swift tug, a float bobs and bait is bought,
Revealing the catch he carefully scoops to admire.
With utmost appreciation for this beautiful breathless bounty,
He only momentarily interrupts this life's pattern,
Before graceful release to the power of the river.
Raindrops do not deter this loyal fisherman;
All around him they fall, creating starburst ripples in tune with the scene.
He breathes in the moment, eyebrows drip refreshing droplets,
As he takes stock of his reassuring inner calm.

Market day

"Three bags for a pound love......they're fresh, don't miss out"
The market stall sellers in fine voice will shout.
The hustle and bustle starts quite early on
And regulars spend till the bargains have gone.
There's tea by the knicker stall, poured from an urn
And Angela's olives sell fast as you turn
Towards sweet shops and pancakes, the pet stall and plants,
Hose pipes and crockery, some powder for ants.
Plump ripe tomatoes, bananas for Sue,
Some socks for our Daniel, and Emily too.
Two bras for Amy, another for Hannah,
Albert's delighted, he's spotted a spanner.
There's baby clothes, blankets, and books by the score
Each Saturday locals are back to buy more.
A patchwork of colour, aroma and sound
A cocktail of various cultures abound.
The scene quaintly organised, buzz in the air,
As people look forward to travelling there.
This market's a comfort, a pleasure, a friend,
No particular need but they will always spend.
When dusk falls a xylophone of sound starts the trend,
Coat hangers and van doors, the boxes they bend.
A medley of songs as they count up the coffers.
And grabbing the stragglers to sell off last offers.
The merchandise carefully into the truck,
In containers for other days, more sales with luck.
And when they've all packed up and 'byes have been said,
The market stall traders make off to their bed.
The scene is now vacant and normal again,
Last empty flower tub pours down the drain.
A crisp packet they missed scurries over the slabs,
Flower seller darts after it, missing her grabs.
So she gives up and smiles as she lets it float on,
All around her is tidy, her work there is done.

Worth the wait

"Harriet, oh Harriet, why this pen my dear?
With all of the Zoo rich with offerings so near,
Your brother's seen tigers and now there's a lion,
It'll be too late when later my shoulder you cry on,
Why are you sitting here? Don't make me shout,
Whatever is in there doesn't want to come out."
But Harriet sat, with determined expression
Patience would teach her a valuable lesson.
She'd seen all the people pour over all pens,
They crowded each fence line and smiled for the lens.
All pens except this one, which mystery surrounded
She'd always been thoughtful, inquisitive, grounded.
She thought if she stayed there till noise had abated,
That she'd be rewarded and so patiently waited.
A snort from grey hut and then snuffly sound
Could be heard from inside, Harriet lay on the ground.
Her heart beating faster, she wondered: What's there?"
And when a wet nose appeared, imagine her stare.
"Hello sleepy creature" she whispered with glee,
"Come show yourself please, no one here, only me."
Two small furry paws, outstretched in sunshine,
Then out in full glory, "Hello PORCUPINE."
Harriet thought "awesome" and watched him walk out,
Drinking and sniffing and strutting about.
"It's been worth the long wait look, look, over here!
His prickles are glistening but nothing to fear.
It helped him to think, choose his moment and see,
He's ok to be out now, he's looking at me."
Her cries of excitement enticed quite a crowd,
Young people to grandmas exclaimed "wow" aloud.
When asked of her favourite, which one did outshine?
Without pausing for breath Harriet cried "PORCUPINE!"

The potting shed

Sturdy walls and bolted door,
Hides inside the garden store.
Plants all watered, groomed and fed,
Their sanctuary, this potting shed.
Seedlings sprouting, wanting sun,
Thinking time once chores are done,
A place to breathe, escape life's pace,
Puts a smile upon your face.
Pack a flask and grab a snack,
'cos once we're in there, life's on track.
From tiny seeds new life begins,
Those tomatoes will be sprouting wings.
Tend to pots with loving care,
Stress release, us being there.
You can travel the world to nourish your head,
But the same can be found in this potting shed.
A quiet retreat, a place to unwind,
Life's riches abound here, of the very best kind.

Unicorn and Popsicles

On a dusty shelf, a pile of books
Tell stories next to teds and trucks.
But while we sleep the magic starts
As pages awake and warm our hearts.
A mermaid sits with flaxen hair
Amongst the pages lying there.
She spies an opening in a book
And slithers down to take a look.
She gasps with joy, adventures born,
Her favourite........it's a unicorn!
The sleepy creature stretches out
As mermaid squeals and flips about.
Then onto feet this mysterious beast
With glistening hooves, for eyes a feast.
"Miss mermaid, I am here for you,
Jump aboard, we've much to do."
Delight as mermaid climbs up high
Winged unicorn then flies through the sky.
Over roof tops where all others sleep
This secret will be theirs to keep.
They leave trail of twinkly stars
Under moonlight as they circle Mars.
A rainbow carpet opens out
In deepest space, mermaid's shout:-
"Yippee...and wow" let's stop awhile
A space picnic creates a smile.
A towering gateau of strawberries and cream
And polka dot Popsicles? What a dream.
They laugh and munch as time ticks on
Then time to go, before night's gone.
Unicorn bows, graceful and strong
And happy little mermaid is singing along.
Soon back at the bookshelf, before anyone sees
Into the books again, but there'll be more nights like these.
When others awaken; all mystery gone
A wink from the mermaid, "see you when sun has shone."

Life

Leaves float down gently and settle in heaps,
At night she walks through them while all the town sleeps.
She ponders the good times, her worries, some sad,
But feelings run deep and life's not so bad.
As she sits there in silence, her seat drenched in dew
Dawn breaks amongst birdsong and green shoots anew.
It's never too late to start over and think
Whatever life deals you, when close to the brink
You should hold onto those good times and keep them in sight
Hold on with your heart, with all of your might.
Life is precious and fleeting, with much to explore
The gift of life's fortunes should not be a chore.
So capture each moment and cherish its truth
Keep smiling with spirit, your spirit, your youth.

Dew drops

This blade of grass, so simple,
Just one amongst the green carpet of lawn.
Touched with additional magic today,
At this waking hour, just after dawn.
A dew drop there so gracefully grips,
Like a jewel glistening at the blade's very tips.
And looking beyond at the rest of the scene,
A myriad more jewels where nature has been.
Behold this stunning display under the tree,
They say that the best things in life are for free.

Race day

Racing post tucked under arms,
Tote booths full of betting charms.
Rippling muscles on fine tuned beasts,
Survey the course in canter,
Amidst an array of colour ablaze,
We hear the jockeys' banter.
Gates are ready, time to line up,
Trap two's the favourite for the cup.
Purple and silver, colour to watch,
Bets are on, some view from box.
Out on terraces though, close to action,
Consumed by atmosphere, magnetic attraction.
Start flags floored, opened gates,
They're off! Shrill cry, air penetrates.
Hooves dig in and jockey's heels,
Are working hard like spinning wheels.
They want the prize, the buzz, their fix,
Some lady's on a lucky six.

"If two comes in, the drink's on me""
It's a worry though, she'll wait and see.
With strength and stealth these horses move,
Like poetry honed from their booth.
Winning post within their sights,
They pound the ground for dizzy heights.
Yellow and blue's a rank outsider,
A neck behind two, and then he's beside her.
Final furlong and a half to go,
Then from the rear's white jersey's show.
Where did he come from? Twenty to one odds,
On the inside now, he's taken it, high flying sods.
With muscles and grace, it's now poetry in motion,
We block out the sound and focus the commotion,
Our eyes fixed on flesh and determined expression,
Nail biting, awesomeness, favourite's lost, what a lesson.
Into winning enclosure, the winner struts in,
The murmur of crowds, sweat pouring from him.
Snorts from huge nostrils and eyes wide, alert,
Another race over and nobody hurt,
The thrill of the ride, aroma of leather,
Back at the boxes the horses all tether.
Jockeys weigh in again, back on their feet,
Celebration time, raise a glass, something to eat?
Race day, nothing like it, crowds outpour,
It's Saturday's ritual, hearts beat once more.

Fine show robin redbreast

When entering the garden space
All birds fly off; on branches pace.
But carefree Robin stays to see
What gifts arrive along with me.
He stands atop a crooked cane
Where hangs a lantern in the rain.
Bird bath collects each rain drop's plop
Robin preens 'neath every drop.
I'm one stride closer... still he stays,
His watching gaze that hardly strays.
I fill the hoppers: brand new seed
Some fat balls hung to quell the greed.
He cocks his head and spies a worm
Swoops in and pulls it, turf and squirm.
But not distracted, soon he's back,
And waiting with his mind on track.
I step aside, and find dry place
To watch his antics! Poise and grace.
This tiny creature, proud as punch.
Flits to and fro...enjoys his lunch.
His feathers glisten, under new ray of sun
Red breast drying off with each darting fresh run.
Cinema? Theatre? Yes...visit we might,
But here at this moment, this beautiful sight
Beats all entertainment we pay so much for
My dear friend the Robin provides so much more.
I make my retreat, with respect, slowly walk,
As others return with a whistle and squark.
I look round in contentment and tally a while
A feast is in motion: I can't help but smile.
And just as I leave this enchanting scene
I'm rewarded as Robin swoops over to preen
So bold and adventurous; my heart skips a beat
As he lands close to hand, scurries over my feet.
Wow, what a picture, this beauty, this might,
Fine show Robin red breast; you're such a delight.

Shakespeare: The Bard of Avon.

With thoughts unleashing at his quill
The master wordsmith's time stands still.
Unrivalled playwright at large today
His resonating words we say.
Unravelled Sonnets still confuse
Was Shakespeare's plan laid to amuse?
We soak up ambience in pleasured awe
World's theatres are unleashing more.
Many a quote is shared in truth,
His poetry educating youth.
"Not of an age, but for all time"
His destiny of verse and rhyme.
A Stratford bairn: his birthplace proud
to raise a man who gave aloud.
He wore his heart upon his sleeve
This noted thespian's dynamic weave
Variety in mood and jest
His early works remain the best.
And as we stroll his streets today
Adjacent Avon's whispering way
Tourists flock to walk the ground
Where Shakespeare's inspiration's found.
Sipping coffee in his space
A captivating thoughtful place.
No amount of ponder will captivate his word,
The Bard provides emotion and a voice forever heard.

Stage fright

Five minute warning, hearts race, curtain fixed,
Backstage they're all waiting, emotions are mixed.
Some holding their breath, others willing the time,
To come sooner not later, nerves over the line.
Two minute warning, the curtain is checked,
Audience muttering, Young Alice perplexed.
One minute warning, get ready to roll,
Audience silent, time taking it's toll.
Time says the clapperboard, "go break a leg,"
But Alice is frozen, directors they beg.
"Please oh please Alice, don't do this again,
We've worked round the clock on this, bad for the brain."
But Alice just stands there and hand claps come slow,
If she doesn't move soon, she'll ruin the show.
Just as the cast members move in for the kill,
Alice is hovering, fighting her will.
Now she is teetering, right on the brink,
"Cut her some slack please and get her a drink."
She steps forward and sighs, and deep breaths gulp inside,
She's out on the stage now, determined eyes wide.
And when it's all over, the last curtain call,
Bravo comes to Alice, cast, audience and all.

Moving day

Boxes packed, it's mayhem here; what to take? I shed a tear.
My home for over forty years, full of dreams, delights and fears.
Moving on to something new, a wrench now that the time is due.
Visiting neighbours who've grown into friends
Bye to the river which cradles garden bends.
Removal van...my life packed in. Throw last pile in rubbish bin.
A hug for Katie from next door. Leave flowers as I mop the floor
And hand made biscuits for those new
I hope this move makes dreams come true.
Down the road I turn around in wonder at this hallowed ground.
Fond memories...I'll cherish these. Brings comfort as I hug my knees.
I wipe my tears.... I'm smiling now. Troubles leaving furrowed brow.
I knew this day was coming soon. I'll be sleeping under the same moon
As all those happenings I hold dear. New home now, my mind is clear.
Last few miles, my heart beats fast, sure, I'll miss my wonderful past,
But almost there, I realise why I made the move and stare at sky.
All the things I want to do. My new beginning, pastures new.
A gasp at van journey's end. New home appears around the bend.
A beaming smile upon my face. I already love this beautiful place.
Boxes file in...one by one. Unpack them till the job is done.
A welcome card and home baked bread.
"A happy place" last owner said.
A knock; new neighbours, shaking hands. Heartfelt trepidation lands.
What an adventure! I'm ready to start.
Memories treasured deep in my heart.

Mince pies

It's March and I'm yearning that feeling you get
When there's buzz in the air, but it's not Christmas yet.
That time when your shopping is not yet complete
You've managed the best of it, with tired hands and feet
It's twelve days before, and friends gather round
When you share your ideas for the photos you found.
You'll wrap one for Deirdre and Jenny and Sam
You'll all sit excited with pickle and ham,
Trimming up trees and a wreath on the door,
Snow falling slowly as mulled wine we pour.
But it's March now, so why must I wait for the time
For more of this merriment, and heady life's chime.
I want to taste pastry that crumbles away
When each bite is taken, Christmas nectar they say.
I want to have moments of wonder, surprise,
This March morning I'll do it...I'll make some mince pies!

Picnic

Alarm clock wakes, a nervous thought,
Pull curtains back, check sunshine's caught.
A sigh of relief and down the stairs,
Breakfast done, away with cares
Sandwiches in foil are wrapped,
Flask and fruit, deck chairs grabbed.
On our way o'er vale and hill
Pass the famous water mill.
Ponder for an hour or two
Relax, unwind, just me and you.
Rare days are these, so savour now
Extinguish every furrowed brow,
And smile as sunbeams come and go
Life's richest fortunes all on show.
Park the car in shaded spot
Blanket out, the flask's still hot.
Bunting tied on trees above
Preparing food with those we love.
Sit back and think of times like these
Hug coffee close, on blended knees
Lie at peace in blades of grass
And watch as sheep and horses pass.
The countryside, our finest gift
Each visit giving us a lift.
When time has come to pack and go,
We cling to these moments we've come to know.
Let's not leave too long a gap
Till next time then, our picnic snap.

Conch shells and salty toes

As I lie here contented with sand in my toes
Sipping sharp lemonade as I screw up my nose.
The breaking tide sprays out its long salty splashes
Which tingle and linger on vulnerable eyelashes.
The pages turn over, at ease with my book
Occasional wandering gaze as I look
At the feast of the ocean before me, right here
A privilege to savour this scene and so near.
No gates blocking views, no noise in the way
I delight in the moment, this beautiful day
No charge for this beauty, this feast comes for free
Can't think of a sight more rewarding to see.
A calming experience; quality time
Reminds me to balance this lifestyle of mine.
We create so much pressure with daily routine
But when all is considered, it's ok to dream.
Lying here at the seaside, seagulls cry is our chorus
Contemplating what's next, what new pleasure before us.
An ice cream with nuts, chocolate flake if you like
A casual stroll or a ride on my bike.
Pashmina round shoulders as evening draws in
Apricot sky provides backdrop and soft sea crashing din.
So peaceful this time by the shore counting shells,
And dreaming of more days like these, breathe in smells
Aromas of coco sun cream and salt in the air
I'm so glad I made time to go travelling there.
A lifetime of days just like these would be great
But all too quickly the day's gone and must go; can't be late.
Work in the morning, it's back with a thud
But this escape from the norm, sure has done me good.

Extra time

In home stand the fans wait with breaths deep and baited,
The whistle can't blow yet, in cold rain how they've waited,
Some say that their football's more than life to them,
So a goal is what's needed now, from long cross it can stem.
The midfield play havoc till tackle kills hope,
This cup game's going full pace, with extra time scope.
The ref blows down hard, it's now two goals a piece.
In terraces shuffling, loud gasps they release.
No time for a pie, watch teams huddled on pitch,
Motivated by managers, bottles kicked to the ditch.
Then onto their feet, in positions they fit,
Though shattered from ninety, they must do their bit,
"Now come on you Reds" the away crowd descends,
With impressive fine voice till the Home crowd then blends,
With their own quirky ditties, some critical, some lame,
Players need motivation to sharpen their game.
With three minutes to go, still no change to the score
There's much nail biting now, some fans leave, want no more.
Then from thirty yards out comes the mother of all passes
It's blue number seven, he's a hit with the lasses.
Over all the midfield and the red number nine,
The ball lands at the feet of young blood, not yet prime,
There's only the goalie to get past, so why
Does he mess up and rocket the ball to the sky?
"Loooser" from the terrace, then quiet again
Fans glued to the action can't cope with the strain.
Goal kick blocked by experience, passed on to the box,
Goalie hops leg to leg after pulling his socks,
He bounces to head off the strike, then he's stunned,
Back of the net is its home now, home hearts beat like drums,
"It's a GOAL" sends a ripple around the home stand
From throats sore with the pressure of how this game panned.
And when ref's final whistle lets out in full song,
They all pour from the terraces, banter flowing and long.
Fans all could be managers, they'd like us to say,
From the timing of subs to the formation of play.
All leading experts, it's their rising, their feast,
It's what makes them all tick, well........on match day at least.

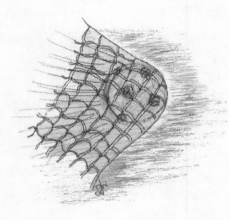

Mr. Moonface

Lucy looked up at the brightly lit sky
Starlight had captured her heart and here's why...
She sat on her window cill hugging her knees
And wished for a jar full of twinkles like these.
Mr. Moonface looked down, beaming magical smile
And then blew her a star kiss which lingered awhile.
The kiss travelled over the star studded sky
Until close up to Lucy who caught it. "Oh my!"
Three beautiful colourful jars had appeared
And each brimful of stardust...how magically weird!
Treasured possessions now, Lucy held tight,
Each jar full of mystery, what a delight!
"Thanks Mr. Moonface"........ A nod and a wave.
"It's my happiest moment....these treasures I'll save."
The jars glowed a brightness like nothing before
As Lucy then dreamed of adventures she saw.
Mr. Moonface looked on as he winked at the jars.
Then smiled as he nestled himself in the stars.
The jars held a thousand more dreams to explore,
For Lucy had wishes worth hankering for.
These magical imaginings are what fun's about,
So shhhhhhhh...keep their secret, don't let it slip out!

Ajar

The doors are closed, there's nobody greeting,
As I scurry down this dusty street.
Just faint mutterings of people and bird's distant tweeting,
As I wonder when somebody I'll meet.
Towards the end, before the turn,
A darkened porch canopy breaks the monotony,
Just one open door sets itself apart
Shafts of light cast shadows toward my inquisitive path.
I consider my options with seconds to spare,
Should I walk on by or stop right there?
Is this a message, should I go in?
I am but a stranger though, by my reckoning.
Be best to just leave it? I am so confused!
If I walk on, none the wiser, other paths I'll pursue.
But to stop here and ponder, could this be my meeting point?
With just my own company for advice, confidence I encourage.
One brave step to the doorstep,
Another to knock......hesitation first.
With clenched fist raised,
I am ready to knock on this mysterious door which stands ajar.
Peeling paint spills onto an unswept floor
And a cobweb wafts gently to and fro in the calming breeze.
I knock just once, palpitations abound.
A cough, and then footsteps approach.

"Yes?" says the old woman, tired and frail, with unkempt hair,
This is where I stumble: What to say? What to do?
So before the gap in conversation widens more,
I respond with a smile. Apprehension, tension,
Is it wrong of me to stop and summon this stranger?
"Hello", then awkward wait.
Her face beams the brightest of smiles,
"Forty three days and seven hours."
To which "pardon?" says I.
"A long time to be silent, so thank you" she says as she closes the door.
And so it was, that there was me,
Decision made I'd been to see,
Someone in need without realising so.
I'll leave her some flowers before I go.
And already I know I'll be visiting more,
Spirits lifted,
satisfied I've not wasted this walk down the dusty street today.
Tomorrow I'll try conversation…so much to explore.

Secrets from a park bench

If only the park bench could talk, one could say,
A myriad of stories we'd share every day.
As passers by ponder to listen or chat,
And friends talk of happenings, love, this and that,
Birds will fly over and perch for a rest
And workers at lunchtime will wipe where they've messed,
The local tramp sleeps there when day turns to night,
Under cardboard he mutters of troubles, his plight.
Morning he's gone again, nowhere to be seen,
The innocent newcomers don't know where he's been.
New strangers sit pondering, sandwich in hand,
And listen through head phones to some favourite band.
A pleasing distraction, and time to reflect,
A meeting point maybe, stay cool, calm, collect.
A bench in the park, so random a place,
And yet thousands of people will here first embrace.
It's a place for forgiveness or clearing the air,
Or for inspired poetry, creativity, flair.
It's somewhere for lovers to commit, say it all,
The park bench has secrets, we'll cherish them all.

Wisdom

The tree trunk
so effortlessly encasing life.
Its sturdy existence protecting its years
and all that it has seen.
The seasons' challenges and gifts…
…harsh winds and icy winters
thawing springs and sunshine hours.
This fellow to be respected is telling a story
each day as we watch him grow.
Let's follow this example that nature has set
and protect what's important; lest we forget.
celebrate those held close and what matters to you
encase and protect, for all else is superfluous.
Happiness is found not in material gain
but through love and thoughtful gesture.
Grow like the tree with stealth and strength
and embrace life's charming moments.
Your reward will be wisdom
profound and enjoyed
and you'll suddenly appreciate the wisdom of others.

Beyond the garden gate

From the sanctuary of home,
A huge wide world beckons,
Filling our heads with hope and our hearts with dreams.
Beyond the garden gate, there's beauty to behold
Adventures to encounter
And boundaries to explore.
With baited breath we consider our journey
It's cost and it's allure.
We ration options, save one or two treasures
Which, with undying passion, we simply MUST do.
Contemplating the calmness of the decision,
Blue seas bashing unpenetrable rocks
Or the scurry of mindset venturing into the unknown
Hills and valleys of winding welcome green....
Whichever way we seek our soul
Beyond the garden gate we'll find it
Before returning home.

Leapfrog

Whilst heading for something, life often chips in
With timely distractions, some full to the brim.
When we start on our journey, we're offered so much
Education, experience, the family touch.
And as we grow stronger down some chosen road
It's easy to lose it, the focus once showed.
So we need to remind ourselves sometimes, it's so,
When we set out our stall for our journey, let's go,
Let's not allow clutter of trivial things
Be true to our destiny, our dreams CAN grow wings.
Leapfrog all those issues that don't matter at all
Continue with ernest, take steps however small.
There's nowt as rewarding as waking each day
With a plan unencumbered and handled YOUR way.
Material things, they can swallow you whole
But we know what's important: to follow our goal.
Looking out for each other is what living's for
Keeping real, grounded, focussed, pretending no more.
Oh what a release when we finally see
The reason for being here, is just to be me.

Photograph

Edges curled over decades of thumbs and ponder,
Creases breaking the spirit of this photograph's song.
This mystery lady who smiled for the lens
Now captures our imagination.
Who is she?
Long flowing locks cradled by her small shoulders,
A fine gown bedecked with intricate smocking and charm.
Tiny fingers grasp a shining suitcase
and an overcoat dangles from her outstretched arm.
Where is she travelling to?
She is holding a letter, its crumpled state enticing our senses in wonder.
Intrigue consumes us as we stare deeper into this enchanting picture.
We may never know her history or from whence she came
But we will continue unheeded
Spurred on by the twinkle in her eye and the perfection of her stature.
We will explore possibility...as we unfold her truth.

Braces for Brian

Day in, day out, it was collar shirt and tie,
Today though, something else had caught Brian by the eye.
At the back of the closet, right there on a hook,
Some bright spotty braces: "Oh let's have a look."
He pulled them out forward into light of new day,
Till Gloria saw them, and couldn't help herself say:-
"No Brian, no please, you wouldn't, would you?"
Spurred on in defiance, Brian knew what to do.
He snapped on those beauties and was taken aback,
"Remember these Glo?" Adding belt off the rack.
"Remember way back, nineteen fifty two,
I'd been plucking up courage to go out with you.
It was on that fine day that you finally said yes,
I was wearing these braces, so they're lucky I guess."
Into her hands Glo's face fell, laughing hard,
"I remember you walking through the gate in the yard,
A right bobby dazzler my mother then said,
As I put on my lipstick, you did turn my head."
So enjoying the moment, a few minutes to spare,
Brian strutted about in the bedroom they share.
"Well, what do you think then, still got it or what?"
"Oh Brian love please, look how they bulge over your pot!"
Brian looked down, he'd a belly, it's true,
But the braces adjusted and round it they grew.
"Right, I'm gonna wear them.........I am, and why not?
Take yourself back Glo...you know that I'm hot!"
Gloria smiled in contentment and said:-
"Come 'ere you daft devil, come back into bed."
So off with all togs, 'cept the braces pants and belt,
He knelt by the bed and his eyes started to melt,
"I love you my Glo, make no mistake about that,
I'm just having you on love, but thanks for the chat.
I know that I'm past it but memory's clear,
I owe it to these braces that I now have you near."
"It wasn't the braces that I went for....not I,
It was everything but'" chuckled Glo with a sigh.
"No, you don't understand dear, I'd struggled for days,
Before taking the plunge, braces helped many ways.

It's like when I wore them they gave me a lift,
And look at us now, you and me, what a gift,"
Well now Gloria cried out with emotional jerk:-
"Go on! Brian wear them...wear them to work."
Without hesitation, he dressed himself fine,
Through mirror he admired finished look, braces shine.
A peck for his Glo and then on with his day,
A fulfilled content Brian in this world today.

A Poet's Privilege

His seat carefully chosen atop rolling green hills
Sharpened pen onto paper; emotionally spills…
All he sees from this viewpoint, with vision and mind
Contentment is flowing as words start to bind.
The poet is poised; his palette enriched
Life's offerings before him, enchanted, bewitched.
Interrupt him? Don't bother; you'll never unmask
This artist at work on his flourishing task.
Furrowed brow now and then as he falters his pace
Until gentle reminders fall over his face.
A smile as he structures the next line or two
With glorious rapture amidst morning's fresh dew.
A profound fine crescendo as lines draw a close
Behold poet's delight as he screws up his nose.
He sits back to admire his victory, his song
Those inclusions were cradled in his mind all along.
His privilege, this creation of purity; an art
He presents now his bounty: a gift from the heart.

Wet paint

A nod so contented, from brush the final jerk,
The painter stands back to admire his work.
The railings look fresh again, to former glory in fact,
Despite the wet paint sign though, " touchers" attract.
What is it about them, this innate need to test?
Do they think the sign's fibbing or having a rest?
They walk up so gingerly, and with cautious hand,
A quick lightening bolt touch, feel wet paint, then eyes panned.
They look all around them, did somebody see?
'Cos now they feel daft, grimace:"not only me.
There's plenty more doing it", and how right they are'
Oh how human race in this way are on par.
We're made of the same stuff, inquisitive nature,
If told a plate's hot, we can't help ourselves either,
We touch it of course to confirm that it's true,
Our in-built cold consciousness driving us through.
So here at the railings, when lunchtime arrives,
The wet paint indelibly touches our lives.
A jacket, a sleeve, a skirt, leg, and a finger,
Paint kisses them all as they lean here to linger.

Puddles

It's a matter of decision
This dank and rainy day
We could decide to stay indoors
And wish the time away
Or we could just embrace it
Raincoats on with no regret
"It's only weather dearie
come on, let's go get wet!"
The puddles are inviting
As we splash and splosh about
Never fails to create laughter
This fun we've found from nowt.
Fresh faced and heads all clearing
Worries gone, complexion bright
And when we're back inside
These smiles will stay with us till night.

The Cruise Ship Ahoy!

I want to go where the cruise ship goes
Where coast lines avail you as you put up your toes.
Sunsets, unencumbered, softly settle for me
As I gaze with contentment way over the sea.
On board I encounter life with slower pace
Sipping wine on the deck with a smile on my face.
Dress up for dinner, and chat among friends
Let all cares leave my head as the journey extends.
Captain's commentary welcome over tannoy this morn
He talks of the dolphins he spotted at dawn…
And tells of the next port we're heading for now.
Grab sunscreen and shades as I mop at my brow.
It's a gem, this vacation, and once I'm unpacked,
My floating hotel has my routine jam packed.
A pleasure each day to encounter new things
Emotional excursions which history brings.
An abundance of cultures and breath taking finds
I soak up the moment, enriched focussed minds.
The crew cover everything, dedication indeed
Somehow pre-empting my every need.
This colourful concoction of fun lifts our hearts
As we sample contentment when each port departs.
I give you the cruise ship; go sample and see
Life's reward for the soul? Well it works great for me.

The Message

With sweated brow, he sweeps the tired street,
Picking up paper bottles and cartons
Cast aside in the wake of daily disregard.
He is familiar with the repetition of what he sees,
Until now...what is the story in this crumpled paper?
With deft accuracy he scoops and continues,
Gathering yet more card, paper and tin.
His curiosity now averted though,
Can he afford to let this message disappear out of sight?
He pushes down hard on the brakes of his cart.
An abrupt halt, and an eager curiosity drives him on.
He seeks out the crumpled message,
And savours it. It sits in his hand and he pauses,
The work of another, these words,
Should he pry?
Or should he allow the privacy of each crease to keep intact their
secret?
As if a myriad watching eyes were upon him,
He glanced sideways, first left and then right.
He slowly unfurled the paper with anticipation.
Then he sat and became consumed in the moment.
"I can't do this on my own" said the note.
"Do what?" He sighed a heavy sigh.
Scouring every centimetre of crumpled space,
He found an engrained imprint of an address.
10 Bemrose Square. So should he stop now?
"Of course not" he thought and without pause or contemplation,
He knew where he was going.
As he pulled up his cart just a few streets away, he looked above the
three steps,
Beyond, a door sat capably blocking him from the intrigue,
Sharp intake of breath and he knocked just once.
First no response and then a voice inside cried out:-
"Not interested" and he knew right then and there,
His conscious decision was alive and right.
"You don't need to do this on your own" he said.
The door opened slowly to reveal her face.
The face of hope, and his enlightened new beginning.

Through a Pumpkin's Eyes

Encased with toughened orange skin
A candle glowing from within
The pumpkin lantern's beam shines bright
This traditional October night.
A masterpiece? Yes, carved with care
A warming face with lasting stare.
What antics makes our hearts skip beat
Tap tap reveals a trick or treat.
Pulses race as spooky ghouls
rattle tins as toffee drools
Crowds stop by to have their fill
sweet treats a never ending spill.
Enchanting shadows fill the wall
It's Halloween, let's have a ball!

Simplicity

The rose, with it's complexity
can fascinate with wonder,
But study petals carefully
creating time to ponder.
Take time to look around you
on the busiest of days,
when in your head you've much to do
Chores tangled in a haze.
Simplify your thoughts in mind
and try not to forget
the little things make brighter days,
Enjoy them; no regret.
Simplicity: a feeling
Your feeling you might say.
For life's better without burden
Life's fleeting, seize the day.

Man's best friend

With caring heart and keenest eye
This trusted friend will not deny
Those times you need a calming thought
He'll be right there: each moment caught.
Patience is his constant
He's content right by your side
Protecting you; always alert
His eyes are open wide.
Returns to home are greeted
With the best welcome hugs of all
Draw a smile as skating paws
Skiddaddles rug in hall!
No one matters more to him
He'll love you, come what may
He senses your emotions
Each and every waking day.
And when he gets his own reward
A walk to local park
He'll display a real affection
for his master; tail wag; bark.
Retiring for the evening
Two paws perched at your toes
That cosy comfort feeling
Brings you warmth. Yes, he just knows.
For there's a word called loyalty
And no friendship can compare
With the love of a dog who simply
Brings you joy by being there.

Windows

Panes of glass all framing
a mix of thoughtful scenes
Encased by a variety
of textures borne from dreams.
Designs present an avenue
for architects to ponder
Shape and size; materials
A picture window over yonder?
Cosy country cottage
Or swanky city pad
Charming townhouse sashes
Or bi folding to be had.
And each one that we meet
Will be quite different from the last
But what a pure delight to notice
Contemporary or past.
Rich heritage to nurture
Or new boundaries to explore
Whichever we encounter
We can always soak up more
Let's linger for a moment
To engage with what we see
Our windows to the future
Reflecting you and me.

Welcome mat

A thousand footprints later
So sorry, frayed and torn
My welcome mat has had its day
It looking quite forlorn.
I've beaten it and swept it
At the start of each new day
But by each closing evening
Once again: in disarray.
I'll need a new replacement
And as I pluck it from its place
It's home for many wearing months;
A smile engulfs my face.
When I think of all those visitors
Who cause the wear and tear
I treasure every moment
Of the times we've come to share
Wiping feet, I let them in
For a natter and some tea
So many special memories
Come flooding back to me.
There are those who visit often
There are those who visit less
But each of them completes my life
With a dose of happiness.
So yes, I'll go and buy a mat
A new one for the floor
Emblazoned with a "Welcome"
For its spot by my front door.
And as its lustre tarnishes
And boots and shoes take toll
I look forward to the wear and tear
friends and family unroll.

Tennis ball

There's a tennis ball on the stairs
It's bright yellow in colour
Casting hues over grey walls and wood.
All around quite in order
Everything in its place
House rules never are misunderstood.
Controversial, then, creative,
This ball being there
We consider it thoughtfully it's colour, it's dare.
So who should pick up on it? Who put it there?
What's the story
And where should it be?
It's one thing to look upon this as some piece of art
A trip hazard though, don't you agree?
It's quirky to find it and then leave be
Not convinced this is right thing to do.
Who'd have thought that an everyday object like this
Could bring out the artist in you.

Attic treasures

For months on end we talked about this day
The usual distractions getting in the way.
If we leave it any longer,
There'll be no more room to spare.
Last time we had a clear out
Hoards of memories we'd share.
Grab a flask, a piece of cake,
We could be there some time.
There's life in them there boxes
All fond memories of mine.
Where to start's the question
So we set about the art
Of sorting out the special things
From which we'll never part.
We knew that this would happen
We started: good intention,
First photograph has got me hooked
A priceless intervention.
A childhood moment by the sea
A memory right there
Stirring emotion just for me
Go on, we've time to spare.
So what if we're distracted?
Sometimes we need a break
To think about good times we've had
A thought, for old time's sake.
A dusty chest reveals a dress
I wore when I was ten.
The detail there within the lace
Hand sewn smocking then.
A bundle in the corner
Wrapped in paper caught our eye
Letters from times at war
We sat, to read and cry.
What treasures these possessions
We could never part with these
Hanging on to every word,
Immersed; let's savour please.
There's love and care between the lines
Heart rending tales of woe

But counter this with happy thoughts
The tenderness they show.
What's that? We say, when digging deep
To the bottom of a pocket
Engraved with hidden message
An exquisite golden locket.
If we had only realised the special moment here
We would have made it sooner
To reminisce about those dear.
Some finds take us to places
We wish we'd never been
Others create smiles about the wonders we have seen.
Underneath a pile of books
Behind cold water store
A dusty covered violin
Could it rise and play once more?
We pluck the strings and tune them well
Before the first fine song
Bring flooding back those school band days
We've saved these all along.
Pass scrapbook please, yes that's the one
My nanna helped me make
Sat patiently with glue and tape
A wonderful, timeless keepsake.
A pause for breath; we look around,
Gulping tea now, from the flask
We laugh, 'cos there's no work been done
We've not even started task!
Surveying o'er all these things
Attic treasures big and small
We wouldn't dream of losing them
Let's savour: keep them all!

Washing line

A gust of wind catches a shirt and two socks,
Charlie's football kit, hanky and all Molly's frocks.
What a story this washing line tells every week
It's all out there in public, theres's no need to speak.
We can see the activity from garments, some small,
Yes, look at them closely now, knickers and all.
There's Barry's best shirt from his job interview,
There's Angela's bra that she left in the loo.
Auntie's best jumper which must be sent back
And Sally's banana suit for fancy dress rack.
There are always the regulars: like dad's favourite pants,
And mum's staple flower dress, she so loves her plants.
Kaleidoscope colours are dancing in time,
To the blusters and ripples of windy day's chime.
Seems a shame then to gather them after such fun
But into the garden we often must run.
The wind turns to rain and if we don't move fast,
They'll drip for another day, like Saturday last.
We'd watched frocks 'a dancin' all covered in spots,
And waited and waited till clouds were just dots.
Sun's timely appearance had just done the trick,
So let's watch today's offering and rescue it quick!

Spellbound

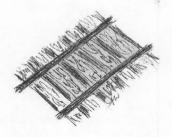

Broadly, her thoughts, they are hankering back
To the days when she'd played as a kid by the track.
As sleepers make rumbles, and rails take the strain,
She knows she"ll be off soon, daily motion again.
But not yet disembarked, she's a memory or two,
To reminisce over, before work is due.
Her mind is decluttered, as if calling to say,
"Don't worry yourself on this journey today,
Focus on moments when heart's made you glad,
Remember the days, all the good times you've had,"
The tracks composition, it's meaningful banter,
Like horse in full gallop, slows down into canter,
And then trots to the junction house, grinds to a holt,
Passengers off like they mean it, some thunderbolt.
Out of the station via shank's, car or bus ,
There's a memory been awakened in every one of us.
Clickety clack, clickety clack, the train's familiar lullaby,
Has captured an emotional venture to mind's eye.
And today is no exception as her feet hit terra firma,
She's been day dreaming of daisy chains until the crowds loud murmur,
Brings her consciously to order, heads for her familiar turnstile,
She contemplates her choice of dreams and walks on with a smile.

Christmas pudding

When the gifts have all been opened
As we gather round the tree
Candles brighten smiling faces
Christmas: time for family.
Hugs and warmest wishes
For those we love the most
Gather round the table
Turkey's ready; raise a toast.
Thankful for our roof
And all beneath its warm embrace
Laughter, song, and stories told
And jokes fly at a pace.
All join in, pull crackers
Make a wish for old times' sake
Each Christmas day, let's celebrate
New memories we make.
And though we're stuffed to bursting
There's always room to add some more
Pour brandy on the pudding
And faces all light up once more.
Spoonfuls full of custard,
or enjoy some brandy sauce
Charades next....and the sofa?
That's for the chef of course!
Settle down and snuggle
Throw all cares away today
And focus on life's precious gift
Family bond is here to stay.

Autumn cascade

As we marvel at the splendour
Of a scene adept in gold
Brown layered over oranges
Delighted, we behold.
Autumnal glows awakening
Shrill breezes set to raid
Those aching creaking branches
Of leaves so rich in shade.
And as the wind whips up a storm
Those leaves which tumble round
Form carpets plush with patterns
As they settle on the ground.
All shapes and sizes mixed as one
No matter from which tree
For they were born to mix and blend
For all eternity.
And we can learn so much from this
As people here on earth
Each of us born so different
Together, life's full worth.
A frenzy for our sweeping brush
But pause a while with me
For nature's Autumn season's
Left a feast for us to see.

Fireside

Let's cuddle by the fireside
This chilly winter night.
Icicles, our outward gaze
Cast a glow in deep moonlight.
There's nothing more rewarding
Than two hands which hug a cup
Of warming brew in fire's glow
Eyes closed to savour sup.
A sigh of sheer indulgence
as we snuggle up some more
Candles flicker gently
Warm as toast right to the core.
Contentment fills our faces
appreciating simple gain
Afforded by a pleasure
For which our love will never wain.

Poppy fields

Eyes all wide, an aura
around those wretched days
When all who bravely fought for us
got tangled in the haze
Tears from weeping mothers
and friends who can't forget
But go ask any soldier
And they'll not display regret
For heroes don't need invites
They're ready with resolve
To go and do their level best
In wars we'll never solve.
And we must all remember those
who gave so much for peace.
so we can live our lives today
Commitment doesn't cease.
The poppy fields will tremble on
The stories often told
November's special time to pause
The memory undersold
For none could truly comprehend
the passion; honour; grit,
We'll try to do them justice
as we talk the tales of it.
But all we humble souls can do
is pay respect to those
who fill our hearts with pride and joy
each year, as feeling grows.
Responsibility is ours
to pass the message on
Remember: gratitude and thanks
To those brave souls now gone.

Patterned lives

Spots and stripes
Ups and downs
Smiles and laughter
Tears and frowns.
Time alone
collecting thoughts
Time together
Fun and sports.
Family vibes
A hug, a kiss
Milestones that
we'll never miss.
Seasons offer
Bright fresh things
To contemplate
and grow new wings.
And as each day
Has been and gone
Reflection works
for getting on.
Tomorrow soon
A brand new day
A patchwork quilt
Is due my way.
Expecting nothing
helps us flow.
Our patterned lives
Enriched, we grow.

Time

A grandfather clock stands proud and tall
The master timekeeper of all
And during busy days we rush
And check our watch before the push
Of chores and tasks; places to be,
The clock face spreads the time for me.
From morning when alarm awakes
Elevenses for coffee breaks
Lunchtime ticks along so quick
And afternoons are never slick
Finish work, a smile: break free!
Time for home; for family
And once inside my own front door
Can't help but check the clock once more
Bolt upstairs; some comfy clothes
Check bedside clock, contentment shows.
Time for tea; fridge of choice
Time the eggs, I'm in full voice
Phone beeps with a text or two
Check the time they sent it through.
Feet up now and telly on
Time for news, all pressure's gone.
Soon bedtime looms to end the day
I'm pleased with what I did today.
What an invention in yesteryear
Pacing ourselves, concise and clear
We owe a lot to each tick tock
The humble irreplaceable clock.

Orchestral city

Some will say a city's buzz
is noisy; aggravating us
But pause a moment, stop and look
Each corner's from a storybook.
Like characters found on every page,
Each pavement gives thought to engage.
From crack of dawn, the sweeper's out
Cleaning streets as voices shout
News stand's been charged with latest views
Coffee in hand, folks stand in queues.
Hum of voices test our ears
Laughter, smiles, debates and fears.
Bakers aroma fills the air
as noses lead us over there.
Men in suits all walking fast
Tapped tunes as ladies' heels walk past.
Hungry shoppers fill their bags
And meet old friends in lunch time lags.
Window cleaners cherry pick
the tower blocks, precision slick.
Air brakes as the buses halt
Disembarking with a jolt,
Moving on, a smile and thanks
To workers on the taxi ranks.
Sunshine warms the pavement machine
As cafes spill, inviting scene.
People watching, just for fun
No boredom here, the day's begun.
The city's orchestra in full view
sights and sound abound for you.

Saving Tommy

Tommy took a tumble
He landed on his head
And now he's having medicine
To mend his weary head.
All bandaged up, our teddy
But we know he'll be back
'Cos he's our faithful special friend
He'll soon be right on track.
All he needs is love and care
A story? Maybe two!
Aw, there, there little Tommy
You know we all love you.

Racing twigs

Backs arched and leaning, yonder bridge
plays host: a fine tradition
For we've been doing this since kids
On many an expedition.
Find a sturdy chirpy stick
And rub it for good luck.
Drop it in the water,
and pray it won't get stuck!
Line up along the water's edge
Encourage only yours
You want your stick to come home first
But then the water pours.
Tumbling with twists and turns
Not knowing who's is who
Oh dear, so who is winning now?
We all know what we'll do
At finish line we all debate
And measure twigs for size
But does it really matter now
Whoever claims the prize?
Tumultuous and dangerous
The river's wending ways
Keep us engaged and occupied
And there'll be other days
To concentrate and have a go
This simple gift of pleasure
Don't ever underestimate
This lasting lifelong treasure.

Village Fete

Potted jam lined up in rows
Engaging sellers tapping toes
Marching band are on at two
And Henry's in Tombola queue.
Sun's come out to help the day
Maisie's grandma leads the way
She'll cut the ribbon... And they're off
Pouring teas, preparing scoff.
Jumble stall is doing well
Rita hopes her cakes will sell.
Fire Engine's lights are on
Pure delight for little John.
Police dogs doing their display,
This gorgeous village fete in May.
What a fabulous summer start
School choir looking very smart
Community out in full force
Do this again next year? Of course!

The Artist

What is art? We may ask.
The answer is complex and yet sublime.
Art is the flourish of ambition on canvas, or an ink drenched quill
at work on an expanse of cartridge so sleek for the eye.
Art is in being, for all that we see becomes sculpture.
A beckoning for creativity.
A fruit seller's counter, so carefully placed.
A child's finger painting, unencumbered by pretext,
just pure; a creation straight from the uncluttered imaginings of his mind.
What is art? We may tell.
For it is vision and conquest.
Masters there are, but who are we to judge?
Can we not find beauty and art in all things?
A potter's deliverance, from kneading with pride.
A blacksmith at work on his craft.
Composition of places and spaces or light.
A fortune before us in everyday life.
What is art? We might see
Surroundings abundant. A glorious rapture in full song
A tapestry of colour created in silk
Or an open minded view of the stars and the sky.
What is art? Here's the answer, for nothing's more sure
Enraptured imaginings. A positive journey, and one we should make
To condition the soul. To understand that there are no boundaries.
Art is what you choose to see and only you should decide
Which elements are your masters. Too many of us draw barriers
A feared encounter? Let us not isolate art to those who think they know
We are all collectors and art is all around us
To enjoy it is to revel in it… intoxicating.
The true artist is sublime indeed.

Seasons of change

Our climate, so taken for granted
We awaken each day to the news
Of a storm or a flood or rain shortage
And we're on with our day, paying dues.
We're distracted from what is important
Let's consider what we need to do.
Let us savour each season's existence
And do justice to provisions anew.
Can't we save the flood water and use it
When there's drought, or the crop loses corn
Oh how I wish answers came easy
But I find myself feeling quite torn.
I soak up the seasons for what they provide
And I love that they change through the year
But I will try in future to preserve
The miracles around me, so near.
I'll quietly bother to notice
The wonders we're given each day
And I'll think of our planet more closely
As I move on enjoying my stay.

Teapot

It's surprising, when calm, to consider
This friend who stays constant and true
No matter, whatever the troubles
Always there to provide a fresh brew.
Listening to all of our worries
Celebrations or something to share
A variety of familiar faces
Will often just pull up a chair.
With hands clasped around a fresh cuppa
There's plenty to talk of each day
Happy moments to chat and laugh over
Sad reflection to ponder our say.
"Good to talk:" we all like this expression
And the talking which tops all the lot?
Precious hours that we share with each other
As we pour from our trusty teapot.

Poetry Distraction

My poetry is such a distraction
Not what you might think this implies
It's there when I wake in the morning
And it lurks till night closes my eyes.
I'm trying to finish my novel
But each time I sit down to write
A poem will enter my head space
Full of promise with structure and might.
So of course I will entertain phrases
Which link in theatrical ways
And dance off the page with a flourish
Enhancing the brightest of days.
A moment to ponder flamboyance
Make it rhyme? Add some intrigue or zest...
Can't declutter encroachment of favour
This one's always apart from the rest.
The best yet, so shall I throw caution
to wind as I finish this text?
Or is that one line will remain an enigma
So shelved, I moved onto the next.
It's true, I have unfinished business
'Work in progress' I think you could say
But each poem I've started has meaning
I'll not rush them; they'll all have their day.
My poetry is such a distraction
And yet it's so giving of thought
I'll not tire from the lines I imagine
As I scribble down what life has taught.

Waterfall

Rugged rock faces are shaped
By nature's sharpest mother tool
A torrent from the waterfall
Startled faces splashed and cool
Rainfall steers the motion
Deciding on the feat
Summer sizzles give a trickle
Winter's plentiful to greet.
This spot provides abundance
Different pictures every time
Determined by the weather
And the pleasure's yours and mine.
Enriched by seasons wonders
Framed with greens or gold or white
Depending on the time of year
Variety to delight.
A visit to the waterfall
Formed an ancient age ago
I'll nurture its full glory
Whether sunshine, rain or snow.
A place to sit and think alone
Or admire whilst hand in hand
As loved ones share the moment
Times like this make life so grand.

Wild horses

Gentle breezes catch flowing manes
Thunderous hooves dance through undulations
Echoes from mossy ground
Of freedom in its most beautiful form.
Distant bands of beasts, poetic in numbers
Approach as dust clouds add mystery...
Closer and closer
Until the rapturous reveal
Of muscle and grace
Halts to inspect our gaze.
Unencumbered by fence or foe
Their steaming stud piles defining their space.
Their contentment sublime,
They inspect us as we, in awe, stand to observe.
Flight is their instinctive defence,
Save the lead stallion, who shows no fear as he looms so close.
Snorts from warmed nostrils
And eyes glistening
as shafts of sunlight capture them like jewels.
Intelligent and inquisitive,
He stomps...
A reminder of his position.
And then, as swift as the clouds
He turns and heads for the horizon,
His bands of followers
Stampede into the sun,
Resplendent coats, sweated,
Unfurl one after another
Until we gasp in their wake...
For a more exquisite sight
Is nowhere to be found
Than the mesmerising scene
Captured by exhilarating wild horses.

About the author

Anita Williams has been writing for over thirty years, and, during this time, has been carefully crafting stories and poems into the treasures we enjoy today. Growing up in a family of book lovers charged her with an exceptional loyalty to the written word. She loves books! Books across many genres, from her early years reading Rudyard Kipling's poetry and stories to today's preferences such as Victoria Hislop. With a passion for creativity and a desire to bring pleasure to her readers, she believes that life should be appreciated to the full, and it is not unusual to find her outdoors. Even the garden summer house becomes a haven for the odd paragraph or two, and here she will often also paint careful illustrations to enhance her written word. Multi-faceted writing is Anita's secret. She prefers to dip in and out of a series of stories and poems as 'works in progress', preferring to revisit them with new snippets she has imagined along the way, in an effort to maximise their impact. A family loving person who multi-tasks each day, Anita is thoroughly enjoying this journey of writing and picture making. Her inspiration is gathered in many ways, be it out walking, reminiscing, enjoying banter around the dining table with family and friends, or by chance encounter with something she notices whilst out socialising or travelling. Intuitive poetry and timeless stories born out of a lifetime of reading and learning; whichever element you feel compelled to encounter, this author will leave you wanting more.

Other poetry books by Anita Williams

Knickerbocker Glory

A fusion of poetry designed to stir the senses full of life's emotions and experiences, delivering thought provoking verses, rhymes and short stories which will touch your heart,

The Very Great Britain in Poetry

Picture yourself on the embankment as the Oxford v Cambridge boat race glides past in 'Cox and rowers' or imagine the conversation in 'Black cab n' banter'. Yes… cream teas, Wimbledon, Shakespeare, Welsh hills and Burns night… You will find them all captured amongst the crevices of this treat in poetry, in celebration of the delights to be found in Great Britain.

Thank you for reading "Poetry Giving" and we do hope that you enjoyed the poems.

Knowing that sales of this book are assisting with fundraising for this extraordinary charity has been an uplifting and rewarding experience, and we have thoroughly enjoyed pulling together the content for you.

We would be delighted if you could spread the word about this book, and in doing so, you will be helping us with our goal to keep missions in the air.

Each Midlands Air Ambulance Charity mission costs thousands of pounds and remember, this dedicated service is totally funded by people like you. 50% of net profits from each book sale contributes to help vital life saving missions.

Keep up to date and join our mailing list at www.writtenwithasmile.com and help others to find out more by leaving a review on Amazon or Goodreads.

Thanks again!

Best wishes,
Anita Williams

About Maac the mascot

Midlands Air Ambulance Charity's popular mascot, 'Maac' the pup paramedic, can be found at fundraising events and schools across the Midlands of England, helping children to learn more about the vitally important life saving service.

To find out more about 'Maac', and the rest of the Midlands Air Ambulance Charity aircrew, visit www.midlandsairambulance.com or find the charity on Facebook or Twitter.

37870575R00057

Made in the USA
Charleston, SC
24 January 2015